EAST LANCASHIRE
RAILWAY BY NIGHT

MIKE HEATH

HALSGROVE

First published in Great Britain in 2009

Copyright © Mike Heath 2009

British Library Cataloguing-in-Publication Data
A CIP record for this title is available from the British Library

ISBN 978 1 84114 902 8

HALSGROVE
Halsgrove House,
Ryelands Industrial Estate,
Bagley Road, Wellington, Somerset TA21 9PZ
Tel: 01823 653777   Fax: 01823 216796
email: sales@halsgrove.com

Part of the Halsgrove group of companies
Information on all Halsgrove titles is available at: www.halsgrove.com

Printed and bound by Grafiche Flaminia, Italy

INTRODUCTION

The East Lancashire Railway, which is based in Bury, began operating regular passenger services in 1987. At that time trains ran between Bury and Ramsbottom, a distance of 4 miles. These services were extended to Rawtenstall five years later and in 2003 an extension at the southern end of the line to Heywood opened.

In a relatively short lifetime the preservation society, assisted by the local authorities, had reopened these lines, restored or totally rebuilt the infrastructure and created an attractive 12-mile long preserved railway that attracts thousands of visitors each year.

Living just a few miles away I have been able to make regular visits to record the line at work, and many of the locomotives that have visited, throughout all seasons, day and night.

Published in 2006 my book, *Railway Moods – The East Lancashire Railway* took the reader on a photographic journey along the line highlighting the wonderfully varied landscape through which it passes and the beautifully restored structures along the way. Here in this unique album the railway is viewed 'after dark' with the emphasis on the motive power that has worked on the line from the reopening back in 1987 up to the present day. Locomotives are portrayed on shed or alongside station platforms under both the basic lighting available or illuminated by specially positioned floodlighting during enthusiast-targeted photo nights.

The images are arranged in chronological order with the results of my earliest attempts at night photography included to provide historical interest.

I have thoroughly enjoyed compiling this collection which has reminded me of the amazing rate of development the railway has undergone. This is made all the more remarkable by the fact that much of it is thanks to a dedicated group of volunteers. I for one am very grateful to them for the pleasure photographing the results of their toil has given me.

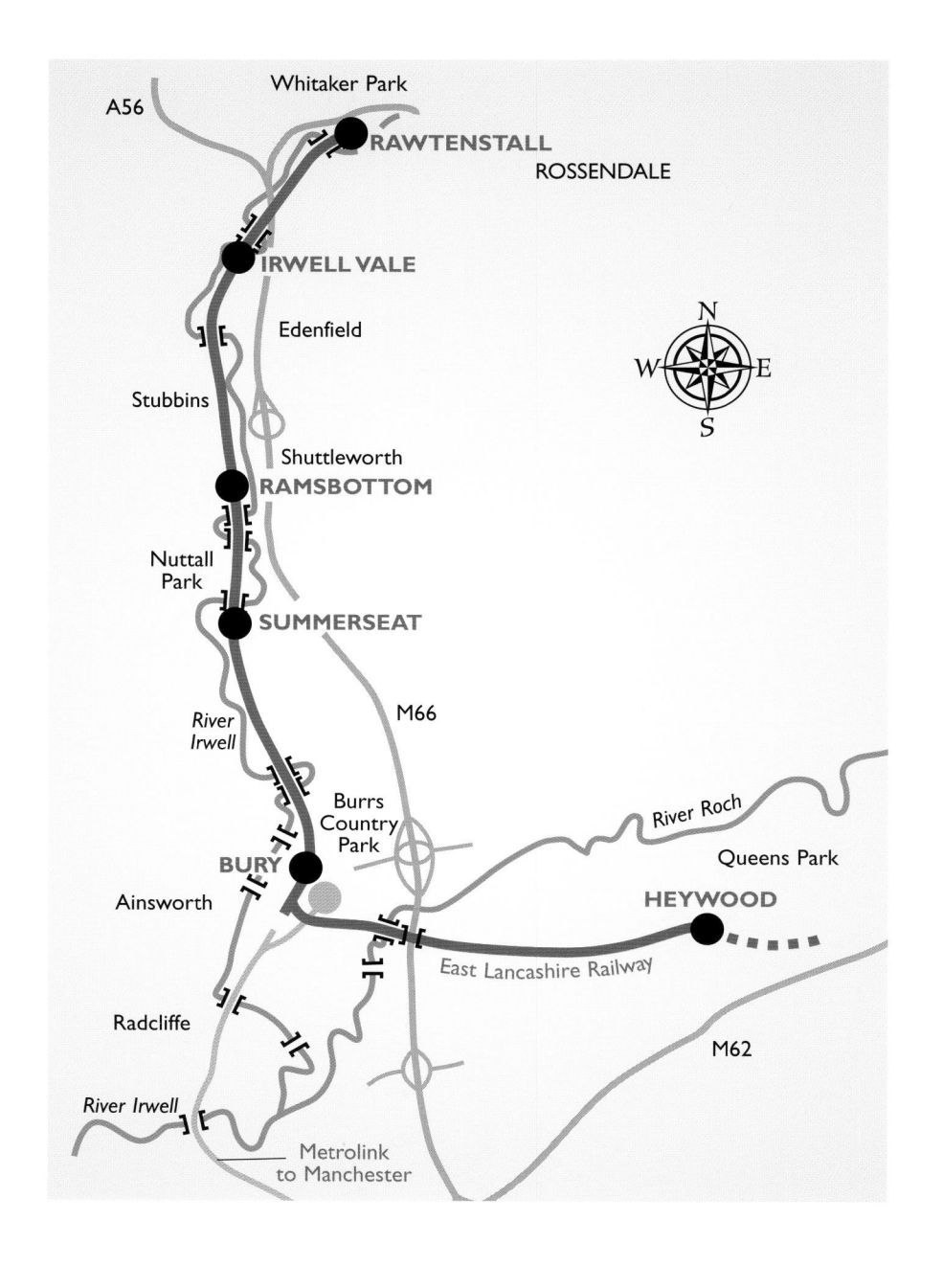

Whitaker Park

A56

RAWTENSTALL

ROSSENDALE

IRWELL VALE

Edenfield

Stubbins

Shuttleworth

RAMSBOTTOM

Nuttall
Park

SUMMERSEAT

*River
Irwell*

N
W E
S

M66

Burrs
Country
Park

River Roch

Queens Park

BURY

HEYWOOD

Ainsworth

East Lancashire Railway

Radcliffe

M62

River Irwell

Metrolink
to Manchester

For most photographers a silhouette at Burrs Country Park utilising the very last of the sunlight would be their final photo of the day. However on many occasions over the last twenty plus years I have returned to the railway, after tea, to capture the East Lancashire Railway by night.

When the East Lancashire Railway first re-opened the southern section between Bury and Ramsbottom on 25 July 1987 ex-industrial tank engines provided the motive power for all services. The winter timetable saw departures after dark enabling me to begin to experiment with night photography. Whilst the composition was satisfactory the home development of the film was not so, with quality deteriorating as the years have gone by.

B.R. Standard Class 4 2–6–0 No. 76079 was the railway's first operational tender engine arriving on the line in August 1989. It had been built at nearby Horwich works in 1957 and was designed to work branch and suburban routes as well as the occasional short haul expresses.

8

At the back end of 1990 a second ex B.R. Standard locomotive, Class 4MT No. 75078, visited Bury having crossed the Pennines from the Keighley and Worth Valley Railway in West Yorkshire.

In January 1991 a 'Standard 4 Weekend' was held during which all passenger services were hauled by one of these two locomotives. So on the Saturday evening I donned my winter coat and with my tripod-mounted Pentax camera made my way to Castlecroft Yard.

The powerful shed-mounted floodlights were a problem but I did manage to find positions where they could be hidden from view and their glow would highlight the outline of the locomotives.

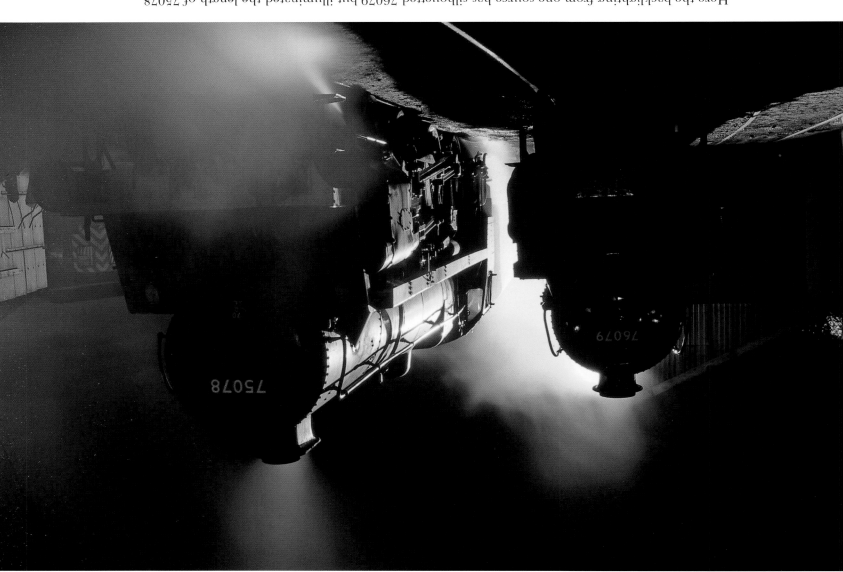

Here the backlighting from one source has silhouetted 76079 but illuminated the length of 75078.

My favourite shot from that evening's effort was this one. The inclusion of the volunteer, with spade, and the ghostly wisps of steam adding to the atmosphere.

Opposite:
For the August 1991 'Big Engine Weekend' Southern Region Merchant Navy Class 4–6–2 No. 35005 'Canadian Pacific' was brought in. Unusually the locomotive arrived facing south offering a different perspective for a Bury-bound train about to leave Ramsbottom at dusk.

In October 1991, Southern Region Battle of Britain Class 4–6–2 No. 34072 '257 Squadron' was temporarily loaned from the North Yorkshire Moors Railway, its home at that time. It saw much use on that year's Santa Specials and was photographed at Ramsbottom on 21 December.

Over the Weekend of 25/26 January 1992 it joined No. 76079 and another 1991 arrival No. 7828 'Odney Manor' for the first 'Big Engine Weekend' of the year.

Great Western Railway
7800 Class 4–6–0
No. 7828 'Odney Manor'
had arrived in February
and was to become a
regular and popular
performer on the railway
for several years.

A fine study of 76079 as it stands alongside the shed on the night of 25 January 1992.

On the evening of 18 September 1992 No. 8 'Sir Robert Peel' was discovered parked alongside the platform at Ramsbottom.

The opportunity was not to be missed and a number of frames were fired off. The glow of the fire lighting the footplate . . . and the burning embers dropping from the fire grate adding interest to the scene.

On another occasion the wet stone paving created a totally different effect and the driver obligingly kept still whilst awaiting the Guard's green light.

Opposite:
No. 34072 with a Bury-bound train as seen from the southern end of the platform.

On the 3 July 1992 'Odney Manor' was the motive power on a Dining Train. At dusk on a summer evening the clear sky retains some colour to fill the background.

An open fire box is the focal point in this reverse angle view.

Another early 1992 visitor from the Keighley and Worth Valley Railway was
'Big Jim' an ex-U.S. Army locomotive which was built by Lima, Ohio, in 1945.

This visit was to take part in one of the railway's 'Big Engine' weekends and the opportunity for some late night photography of this unusual locomotive in the yard at Castlecroft could not be ignored.

The railway's first 'Great Western Weekend' took place on 14/15 November 1992 and the trio of partaking locomotives were photographed under the yard lighting . . .

Opposite: . . . and with illumination from some temporary floodlights.

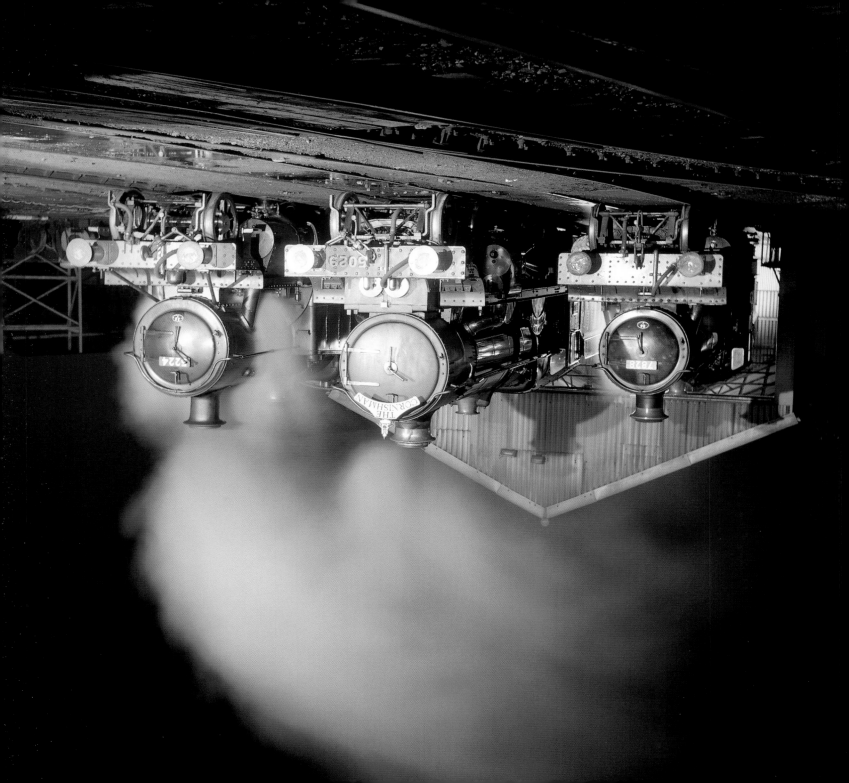

At the time the railway was playing host to former Great Western thoroughbred, 4073 Class 4-6-0 No. 5029 'Nunney Castle'. This was a product of the Swindon Works emerging in 1938 and had been withdrawn from service in 1963. It then languished in Barry scrapyard for thirteen years before being purchased for preservation by the Didcot Railway Centre near Oxford.

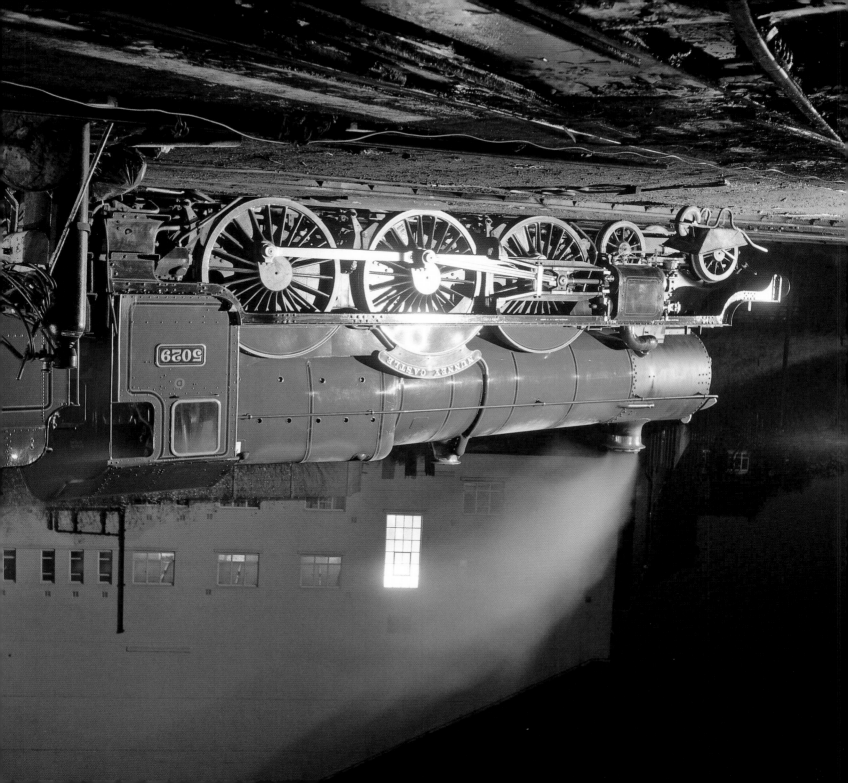

Ex G.W.R. 5205 Class 2–8–0T No. 5224 had just arrived at Bury. Built at Swindon in 1924, withdrawn by British Railways in 1963, and rescued from the scrapyard in Barry Island in 1968 she had been restored by the Great Central Railway in Leicestershire.

Another locomotive to take up residence on the line in 1992 was L.M.S. Class 4F 0-6-0 No. 4422. Built at Derby Works in 1927 to a Midland Railway design first introduced in 1911, the locomotive had been restored to operating condition by a private group at the North Staffordshire Railway, Cheddleton, now known as the Churnet Valley Railway.

In January 1993 it joined 'Odney Manor' and 'Nunney Castle' for the Winter Gala.

February 1993 was a landmark in the development of the East Lancashire Railway
as it played host to the world famous locomotive 'Flying Scotsman'.

The 'Scotsman' was in service every weekend that month including a number of Friday night specials. So it was off to Ramsbottom Station to capture this magnificent locomotive from every angle.

This rear three-quarter shot was made all the more atmospheric with the exhaust steam hanging in the air.

On the main platform the addition of floodlighting from the station building added colour to this portrait.

A sudden downpour created a glass-like surface to the flagstone paving with the reflected light picking out every detail of the motion. A splendid night for photography and my recollection is that I was the only photographer there!

By the end of 1992 the locomotive department had relocated to the former ex-British Rail Electric Car shops at Buckley Wells. August 1993 was the 25th anniversary of the end of steam on British Rail and the railway courageously organised a Steam Festival to commemorate the event and a vast number of locomotives were hired in to join the festivities.

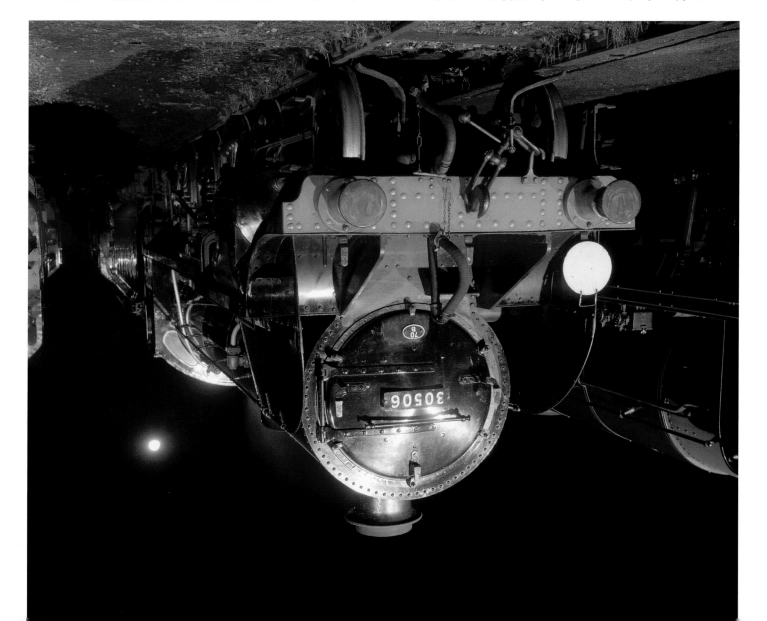

Making the journey from the Mid-Hants Railway was Southern Railway Class S15 4–6–0 No 30506. A 1920 product of the Eastleigh Locomotive works its plied its trade on Southern metals until withdrawal in January 1964. Purchased by the Urie Locomotive Society in 1973 restoration was carried out in stages with an eventual return to steam in 1987. At the time of writing this locomotive is undergoing a heavy overhaul.

'Canadian Pacific' returned this time facing the more usual north. Its working life ran from October 1942 until withdrawal in October 1965. Having languished in the Barry scrapyard until 1973, it initially spent time at Carnforth before moving to Quorn on the Great Central Railway where restoration was completed in November 1990. Like 30506 it is now based on the Mid-Hants Railway.

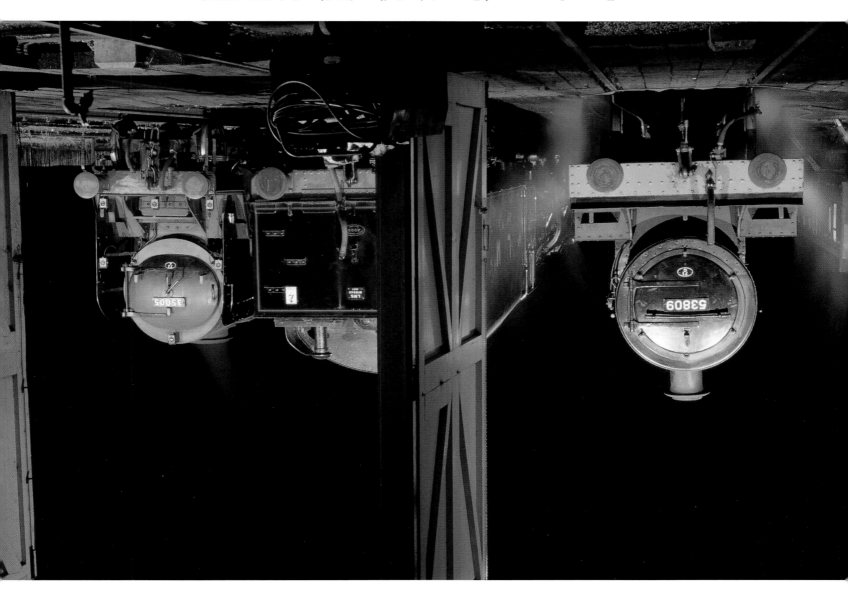

Former Somerset and Dorset Joint Railway 7F Class 2–8–0 No 53809 visited from the Midland Railway Centre in Derbyshire . . .

. . . and with the freedom of the yard a few photographs were taken from just within the sheds.

Two representatives of the 'Jubilee' Class also worked the line during the month long event. Built by the North British Locomotive Company, Glasgow No. 45596 'Bahamas' entered service at Crewe North shed in January 1935. Equipped with a double chimney and blastpipe it remained in use until withdrawal, from Stockport Edgeley, in July 1966. The Bahamas Locomotive Society had by then raised enough money to purchase the locomotive from British Railways. It is currently stored at their base on the Keighley and Worth Valley Railway awaiting overhaul.

Opposite:
Built in 1934 No. 5593 'Kolhapur' was one of a trio of 'Jubilees' that worked out of Leeds Holbeck shed and lasted in traffic until 1967. On 27 August 1993 its London Midland and Scottish lake crimson livery stood out under the lights as it lined up behind the Brunswick Green British Railway liveried 'Bahamas'.

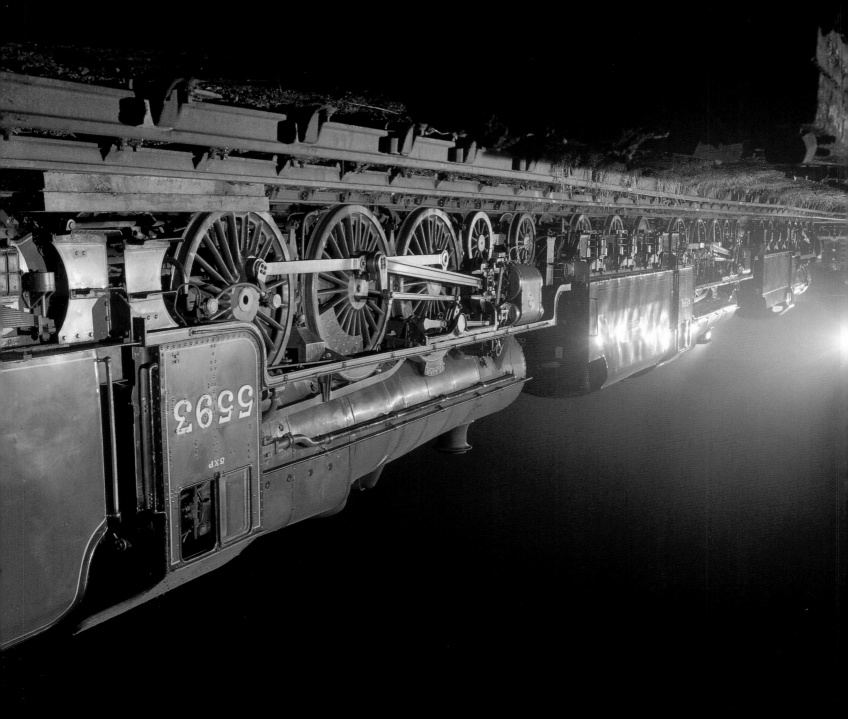

Following successful running-in trials, after a lengthy rebuild from scrapyard condition, former L.M.S. Class 5MT 2–6–0 No. 2765 entered service in January 1994 and took part in the railway's L.M.S. weekend at the end of that month. On the evening of 28 January 1994 it was photographed at rest in the yard sporting British Railway livery and number.

Sharing duties that weekend was 'Black Five' No. 5407 which had been brought in the previous year for the August event and has been a regular performer both on the railway and on mainline specials ever since.

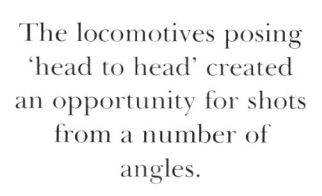

The locomotives posing 'head to head' created an opportunity for shots from a number of angles.

Another main line certified locomotive, Ivatt Class 2 No. 46441, was also hauling trains that weekend.

The 'Duke', as it is affectionately known, had the distinction of being the first steam locomotive to arrive at the railway under its own steam from British Rail at Castleton via the Heywood line.

Opposite:
The Enthusiast Weekend held on 26/27 February 1994 saw more visitors in the shape of Great Western Railway 2–8–0 Tank No. 5224, and No. 71000 'Duke of Gloucester'.

Opposite:
Former Great Western 7800
Class 4–6–0 No. 7828 'Odney Manor'
had been on the railway since
February 1991 and was the first
tender loco to be based on the East
Lancashire Railway on any kind of
long term arrangement. When
photographed on 11 August 1994
it was carrying the ex B.R. Green
livery that had been applied
earlier that year following its
10-yearly boiler overhaul.

Also on shed that evening was North
Eastern Railway Class H 0-4-0 No
1310 which was built in 1891 at the
N.E.R. Gateshead works for
employment shunting the docks.
It was visiting from its preservation
base, the Middleton Railway in Leeds.

On that same night,
18 August 1994, 'Clun Castle',
'Odney Manor', and 5407 provided
an atmospheric backdrop.

Opposite:
One week later and an impostor
occupied pole position in front of the
sheds. Jubilee locomotive No. 5593
'Kolhapur' had returned from the
Birmingham Railway Museum in the
guise of No. 5552 'Silver Jubilee'
wearing the black and silver livery
of the class doyen.

The October 1994 event saw the arrival of British Railways 9F No. 92203 which was one of 251 class 2-10-0s built to the design of R.A.Riddles as the standard 'heavy freight' locomotive for British Railways. 92203 was built at Swindon Works in January 1959 and was working the heavy iron ore trains out of Liverpool docks to Shotton Steel Works when it was taken out of service after hauling the last steam-hauled ore train in November 1967.

Its owner is the famous
wildlife and locomotive
artist David Sheperd.
He purchased it
straight out of
BR service and
subsequently gave it
the name
'Black Prince'.

My recollection is that the 9F arrived late on the Saturday of the Enthusiasts' Weekend and was steamed that evening to join, amongst others, L.M.S. Jubilee locomotive No. 45596 'Bahamas' and Black 5 No. 5407 on Sunday's duties.

Over the weekend of 25/26 February 1995 the Black 5 and Jubilee were photographed forming a protective ring around former Great Western Railway 0-6-0 Pannier Tank No. 7752 which had wandered many miles from its Birmingham Railway Museum home.

That same month saw 5407 alongside 'Duke of Gloucester' and 'Sir Nigel Gresley' and what a stunning sight they made under the lights!

On an extremely cold 27 January 1996 I called in at Ramsbottom Station and from very near the welcoming brazier took just this one photograph. Note the wisps of steam from each of the carriages denoting the steam heating in full working order. (I would have moved the traffic cone but it was frozen to the spot!)

It was obviously much warmer on this particular evening as the station staff have ventured on to the platform!

The 1996 February
event witnessed a liaison
between the 'Duke of
Gloucester' and the
'Duchess of Hamilton'.

Another occasion where after taking the 'popular' photograph alongside the throng of fellow enthusiasts I ventured into the yard for the reverse shot.

Opposite:
'Sir Nigel Gresley' completed the line up.

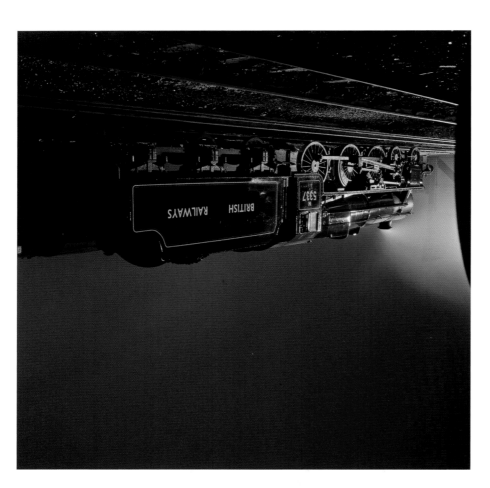

Black Five No. 45337 had arrived at Bury in 1984 and underwent a complete restoration before returning to steam in May 1995. It holds the honour of being the first tender engine completely rebuilt at Bury and the first of the class to be steamed, having been rescued from the famous Barry Island scrapyard. Here it was captured, at Buckley Wells, in ex-works condition on the 28 September 1996

Opposite:
The A4 first visited in 1994 returning a year later for an extended stay on the line making Bury its temporary base between main line excursions and visits to other preserved railways.

In its first year of operation it had carried a temporary basic black livery and the No. 45337. However when the time came to apply the final paintwork its owning group decided that the early British Railways livery should be adopted. The prefix 'M' denoted Midland Region. On the 26 January 1997 the locomotive was photographed at Ramsbottom on that evening's diner service.

A Deltic Weekend was held over 7 and 8 March 1997 and the three stars of the show were lined up for photographers on the Saturday evening. From left to right are 55015 'Tulyar', 55002 'King's Own Yorkshire Light Infantry' and D9019 'Royal Highland Fusilier'. British Railways named each of the Deltics after either a famous regiment or, as is the case with 55015, a race horse. In 1952 'Tulyar' had won the Derby, Eclipse Stakes and St Leger races. (That's the horse not the diesel!)

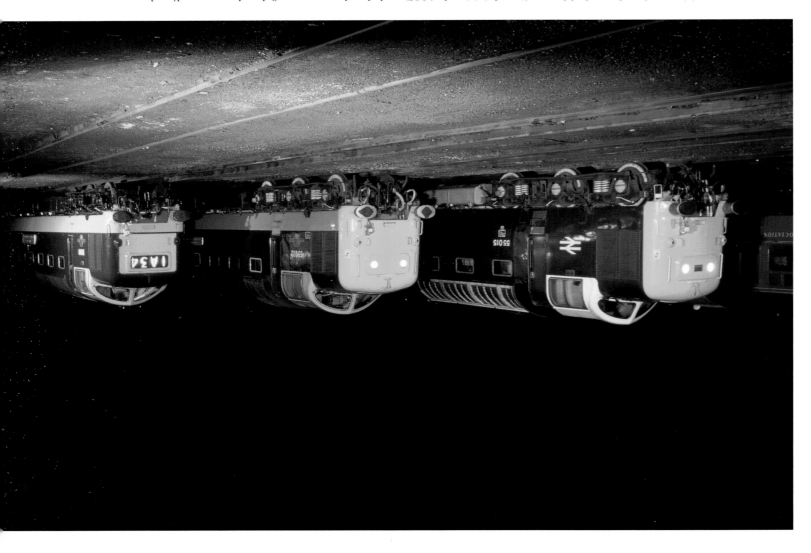

The 1998 season saw 46229 'Duchess of Hamilton' making public appearances in Brunswick Green having been temporarily repainted with special permission from its owners the National Railway Museum. It made a stirring sight at dusk on the 25 January.

It was January 2000 before my next nocturnal trip to the sheds
attracted by the presence of two more visitors to the line.

West Country Pacific 34027 'Taw Valley' had based itself at Bury between mainline duties whilst LNER Pacific 60532 'Blue Peter' was spending a few months on the line courtesy of its owning group, the North Eastern Locomotive Preservation Group (NELPG). The line up was completed by Black Five No. 45337 disguised as No. 45156 'Ayrshire Yeomanry'. (Photos Karl Heath)

By 11 March 2000 No. 45337 had forsaken its disguise.

Saturday 27 January 2001 and another visit to Ramsbottom Station and another locomotive in disguise. This time Black 5 No. 45407 had taken on the identity of 45157 'The Glasgow Highlander' and was taking part in that month's enthusiasts' event.

Once the Bury-bound train had departed it was over the footbridge to
capture the double-header with both locomotives having plenty of steam to spare.

A little later 'Green Arrow', also with a full head of steam, was preparing to continue the journey back to Bury.

One month later and both the Black 5 and this photographer were out of doors during a surprise snow storm. Whilst Bury itself received a sprinkling, the northern terminus suffered a much more substantial covering.

There were not many passengers stretching their legs that night! (Photos Karl Heath)

28 October 2001 and visiting 9F No. 92212 has just arrived at Ramsbottom with the last Bury – Rawtenstall train of the day.

It was to be another two years before my next nocturnal sojurn on the railway. The October 2003 Enthusiasts' Weekend included an organised photo evening at Bolton Street Station.

L.M.S. No. 5690 'Leander' was one of two locomotives
that took up a number of positions around the station.

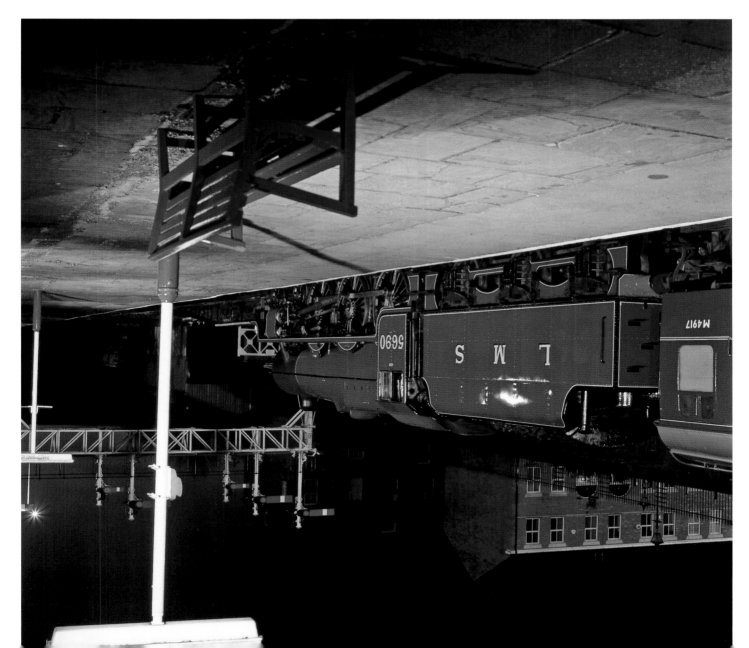

The second was a visitor from the North Yorkshire Moors Railway, the former North Eastern Railway J27 No. 2392.

83

The J27, complete with
freight stock was initially
positioned beneath the
then new signal gantry
at the south end of the
platform . . .

. . . before pulling into
the station alongside
platform 3 . . .

. . . allowing the guard to take a comfort break!

87

The final movement saw the locomotive under the station canopy.

These organised evenings do allow you to capture the subject from a number of angles and the inclusion of working members in period uniforms certainly adds to the atmosphere.

Over the next few years my commitment to the publishers Halsgrove, which was initially to produce three titles for publication in 2005 saw a further five emerging over the following three years! This left little time to visit Bury; however, the January 2008 'winter gala' saw an incredible line-up of visiting locomotives and the night shoots proved too tempting.

The Friday night event was centred on the Buckley Wells shed yard which now benefited from additional column lighting and extended sidings as a result of a private contractor utilising the area during their re-laying works on the Manchester Metrolink system. The National Railway Museum-owned ex-LNER 2–6–2 No. 4771 stood head to head with 71000 'Duke of Gloucester'.

'Green Arrow' was making its last ELR Gala appearance as later in the year it was due to be withdrawn at the end of its boiler ticket, with no plans for further restoration in the foreseeable future.

Former London Midland and Scottish locomotive No. 5690 'Leander' was again in residence . . .

'. . . along with another ex-LMS locomotive, 4-6-2 No. 6201 'Princess Elizabeth'.

The Great Western Railway was represented by 1929-built No. 4936 'Kinlet Hall' standing next to 9F No. 92214 a relative youngster dating from the last years of British Railways.

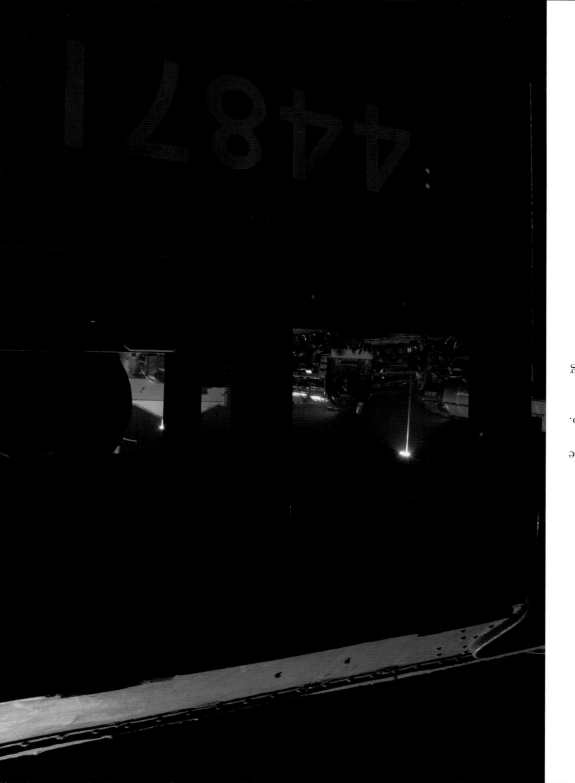

Again in search of that different angle a reasonably successful attempt was made to use the cab of Black Five No. 44871 as a frame. This locomotive had worked right up to the last day of steam in 1968 and was undergoing restoration.

The following night all activities were alongside the platforms in Bolton Street Station.

'With the signal gantry providing a striking frame for, 'Duke of Gloucester' . . .

. . . and a fire escape staircase to an adjacent
office block offering a different perspective.

Later that evening the 'Duke' and the 'Princess' were captured side by side.

The volunteer crew and staff entering the spirit of the evening by agreeing to keep as still as possible for several seconds.

Now that the digital age of photography is upon us it is easy to forget the impact that black and white images can have with railways being a particularly good subject, especially at night. So over the next few pages I present a further selection from that weekend converted to monochrome.

March 2008 saw me unusually attracted to the Diesel Fraternity's 'Night Rider'
Gala event where trains operate throughout the night. Initially I set up at Rawtenstall
to witness the arrival of Class 55 Deltic 55022 'Royal Scots Grey'.

Watching it run round its train, pausing momentarily whilst the points were changed.

Passing through Bury on my way home I noticed that there were
locomotives posed with their trains in the station. Therefore a slight detour was called for.

Class 40 D335 was awaiting the 'right of way' at the southern end of platform 2 . . .

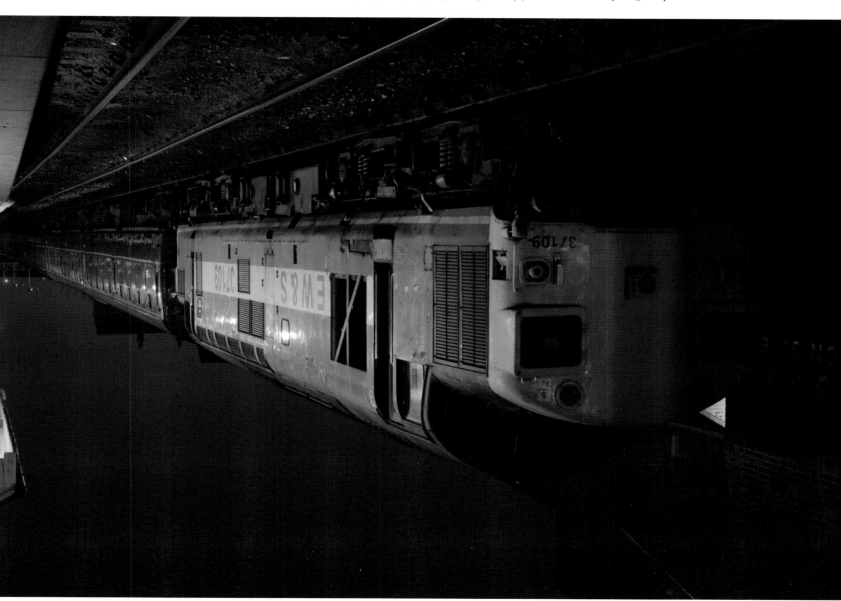

. . . but faced a tug-o-war with newly arrived Class 37 37109 at the northern end of the train.

Platform 4 played host to Class 33 33109 'Captain Bill Smith RNR', a locomotive that had
just emerged following seven years of storage and was to become a regular performer on the line.

Class 47 'Gateshead'
brought up the rear.

With the exception of the plastic dustbin and liner these photographs could have been taken over fifty years ago.

October 2007 and another photography evening at Buckley Wells allowed me to capture a number of locomotives not yet represented in my 'after dark' portfolio. The 1896-built Lancashire and Yorkshire 'A' Class 0–6–0 No 1300 was paraded alongside an impressive collection of well-used fire irons . . .

Opposite:
. . . and shoulder to shoulder with 'Duke of Gloucester'. Making up the trio outside the sheds was a recent arrival at the railway, an Austerity 0-6-0 Saddletank which had spent much of its working life on the Wemyss Private Railway in East Fife, Scotland. It carries the brown livery of that railway.

Two other night time photo 'firsts' were on view that evening. The railway's own 'Jinty' No. 47324 and the visiting Gresley K4 2–6–0 No. 61994 'The Great Marquess'. Making up this particular line-up was Standard 4 2–6–0 No. 76079 in the guise of a class mate that had been based at the Fort William Shed in B.R. days. The loco had carried this number for a series of chartered trains in the west of Scotland and had just returned to the railway . . .

. . . in the company of Black Five No. 45407 that was carrying a red-backed smokebox number, another Scottish trait.

A further selection of shots from that evening converted to black and white.

119

On selected evenings throughout the year the 'Red Rose Diner' trains are run offering passengers the opportunity to enjoy a meal in Pullman-style coaches hauled by a vintage steam locomotive. (I can thoroughly recommend these, they are a great night out.)

On arrival at Rawtenstall diners are welcome to take a stroll along the platform to view the footplate . . .

. . . and admire the station buildings which were built by the preservation society in
an original style, including a clock tower similar to that at Bury's Bolton Street Station.

On this particular damp evening with temperatures hovering around freezing there were not many hardy souls venturing out to watch that evening's locomotive, 'Jinty' No. 47324, running round the train.

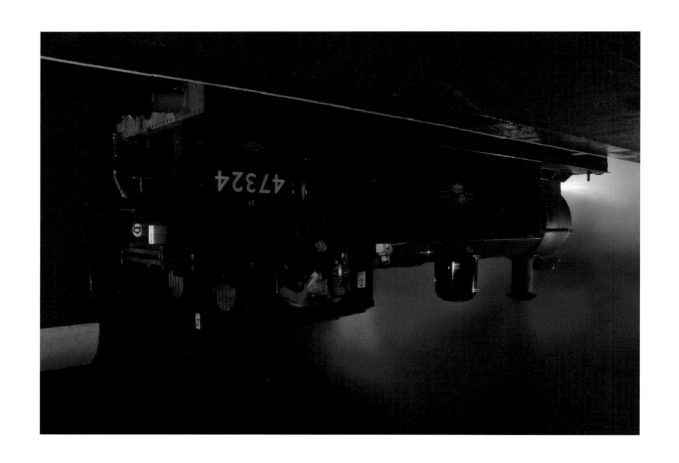

In 2008 the main station building at Ramsbottom, which the society had completed in 1989, acquired a canopy.

Opposite:
With all carriage doors secured it's just a matter of minutes before this 'Special' will be on its way back to Bury.

The canopy trusses and frame were constructed from pieces saved from a number of North West stations but the columns recovered were so corroded that moulded look-alikes were made and erected with a steel column spine to take the weight.

There is a real 1950s feel to the station and for those individuals worried about weighing themselves there is a remedy available locally!!

A little light reading between trains.
The signal box, footbridge and level
crossing all adding to the general ambience.

At the end of November 2008 steam services were handled by visiting locomotive 'The Great Marquess' seen here with a dusk departure.

The last train back to Bury on that Saturday was, as per usual, diesel hauled.

As with most preserved railways the final events of the year are the Santa Specials which operate each December weekend. The Booking Hall and covered footbridge are beautifully decked out with festive lighting.

Whilst taking these photographs all I could hear was 'WOW' accompanied by a sharp intake of breath as, children and adults alike, arrived for their magical journey.

Down on the platform excited children, of all ages, await the arrival of the train. During Santa season the railway operates 'Shoppers Shuttles' to and from Heywood, hence the DMU alongside platform 1.

Santa is about to board the train to distribute presents during the return journey to Ramsbottom.

At Ramsbottom there is a diesel-hauled shuttle service operating to Rawtenstall.

The final 'Santa' trains of 2008 were hauled by Black Five No. 45231 'The Sherwood Forrester'.

It made a fine sight under the canopy…

...and the lights illuminated the side of the locomotive perfectly. (Photo Karl Heath)

The street lighting that has coloured up the stone paving was actually so effectively a big photographic problem causing excessive flare. Very careful positioning was required to frame the locomotive beneath the waiting shelter canopy which in turn hid the strong street lamps from view. A night photographer's lot is not an easy one!

(Photo Karl Heath)

Back at Bury the locomotive arouses the interest of what the preservation movement as a whole hopes will be a working volunteer of the future. (Photo Karl Heath)